Languages of the World

Urdu

Lucia Raatma
Naresh Sharma

Heinemann Library
Chicago, Illinois

www.heinemannraintree.com
Visit our website to find out more information about Heinemann-Raintree books.

To order:
☎ Phone 888-454-2279
💻 Visit www.heinemannraintree.com to browse our catalog and order online.

©2012 Heinemann Library
an imprint of Capstone Global Library, LLC
Chicago, Illinois

Edited by Dan Nunn, Rebecca Rissman, and
   Catherine Veitch
Designed by Marcus Bell
Picture research by Ruth Blair
Production by Victoria Fitzgerald
Originated by Capstone Global Library Ltd
Printed and bound in China by South China Printing
   Company Ltd

15 14 13 12 11
10 9 8 7 6 5 4 3 2 1

Library of Congress Cataloging-in-Publication Data
Raatma, Lucia.
   Urdu / Lucia Tarbox Raatma and Naresh Sharma
      p. cm.—(Languages of the world)
   Includes bibliographical references and index.
   ISBN 978-1-4329-5082-8—ISBN 978-1-4329-5089-7 (pbk.) 1. Urdu language—Textbooks for foreign speakers—English. 2. Urdu language—Grammar. 3. Urdu language—Spoken Urdu. I. Sharma, Naresh. II. Title.
   PK1973.R33 2011
   491.4'3982421—dc22   2010043788

Acknowledgments

We would like to thank the following for permission to reproduce photographs: Alamy pp. 6 (© Jon Parker Lee), 10 (© Picture Contact BV), 14 (© MBI), 22 (© Idris Ahmed), 29 (© Neil McAllister); Corbis pp. 9 (© Steve Hix/Somos Images), 12 (© epa), 19 (© Annie Griffiths Belt), 20 (© Galen Rowell), 23 (© Jonathan Blair), 26 (© Matiullah Achakzai/epa); iStockphoto pp. 15 (© Pathathai Chungyam); Photolibrary p. 18 (Bill Stevenson); Shutterstock pp. 5 (© Asianet-Pakistan), 7 (© afaizal), 8 (© aspen rock), 11 (© Marilyn Barbone), 13 (© michaeljung), 15, 21 (© ansar80), 17 (© Arvind Balaraman), 24 (© zeber), 25 (© JeremyRichards), 27 (© Eva Gruendemann), 28 (© JeremyRichards).

Cover photograph of Indian boy reproduced with permission of Shutterstock (© Rohit Seth).

We would like to thank Naresh Sharma for his invaluable help in the preparation of this book.

Every effort has been made to contact copyright holders of material reproduced in this book. Any omissions will be rectified in subsequent printings if notice is given to the publisher.

All the Internet addresses (URLs) given in this book were valid at the time of going to press. However, due to the dynamic nature of the Internet, some addresses may have changed, or sites may have changed or ceased to exist since publication. While the author and publisher regret any inconvenience this may cause readers, no responsibility for any such changes can be accepted by either the author or the publisher.

Contents

Urdu words are in italics, *like this*. You can find out how to say them by looking in the pronunciation guide.

Urdu Around the World

The Urdu language is spoken all over the world. It is one of the main languages of Pakistan. Urdu is also one of the languages of India. Pakistan and India are both in Asia.

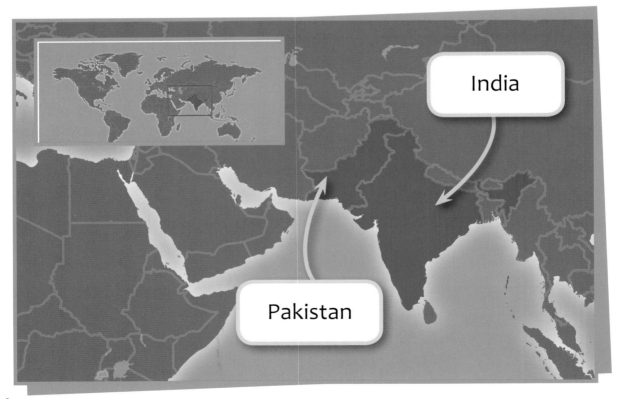

India

Pakistan

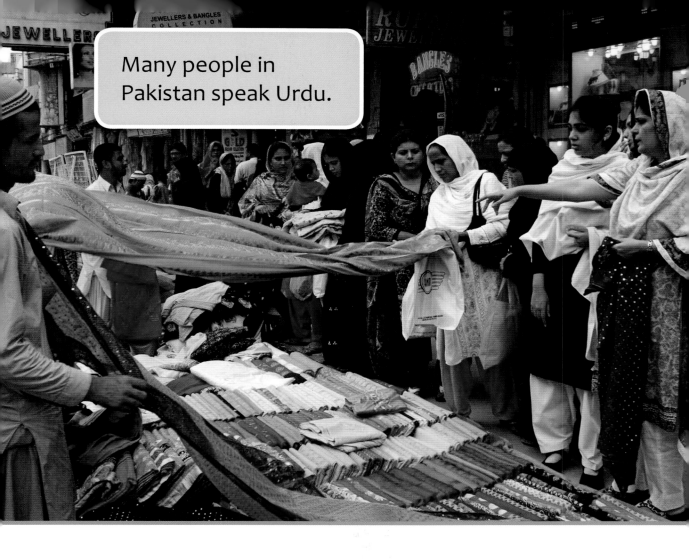

Many people in Pakistan speak Urdu.

People in many other countries speak Urdu, too. Urdu speakers can be found in Afghanistan, Australia, South Africa, the United States, Germany, the United Kingdom, and other places.

Who Speaks Urdu?

Throughout the world there are about 100 million Urdu speakers. Around 400,000 of those live in the United Kingdom. The United States is home to more than 250,000 Urdu speakers.

Urdu is spoken by many people outside Pakistan.

In Saudi Arabia, thousands of people speak Urdu.

In India, almost 50 million people speak Urdu. Around 11 million Urdu speakers live in Pakistan. Saudi Arabia has many thousands of Urdu speakers, too.

Urdu and English

You may already know some Urdu words. Some of them have become part of the English language. For example, *khaki* comes from the Urdu language. It means "dust-colored."

Khakis are named after a color in the Urdu language.

"Pajamas" is a word that came from the Urdu word *pājāmā*.

The English word "pajamas" comes from the Urdu word *pājāmā*. If something is easy or soft, we might say it's cushy. That comes from the Urdu word *khushī*, which means happiness.

Learning Urdu

The Urdu alphabet is very different from the alphabet used to write English. It is read from right to left. There are 39 basic letters, and 13 extra ones.

The Urdu alphabet is very different from the English one.

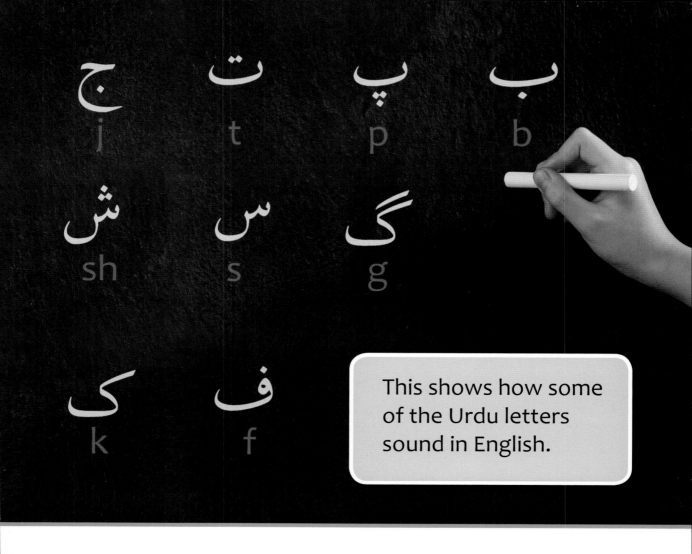

ج j   ت t   پ p   ب b

ش sh   س s   گ g

ک k   ف f

This shows how some of the Urdu letters sound in English.

In this book Urdu words are written in the same alphabet that is used to write English. This makes them easier for you to read. The extra marks on some of the letters show how the words should sound.

Saying Hello and Goodbye

In Pakistan, men may shake hands with each other when they meet. If they know each other well, they may hug. Women often hug and kiss when they meet.

How to say it

hello = *assalām ālekum*
goodnight = *shab bākhair*
goodbye = *khudā hāfiz*

An Urdu speaker might say "*assalām ālekum*" ("hello") or "*subha bākhair*" ("good morning"). Later, he might say "*shab bākhair*" ("goodnight") and "*khudā hāfiz*" ("goodbye").

Talking About Yourself

When you meet someone new you might say "*Āp se milkar khushī huī*" ("Pleased to meet you"). Then you might say "*Merā nām Lucia hai*" ("My name is Lucia").

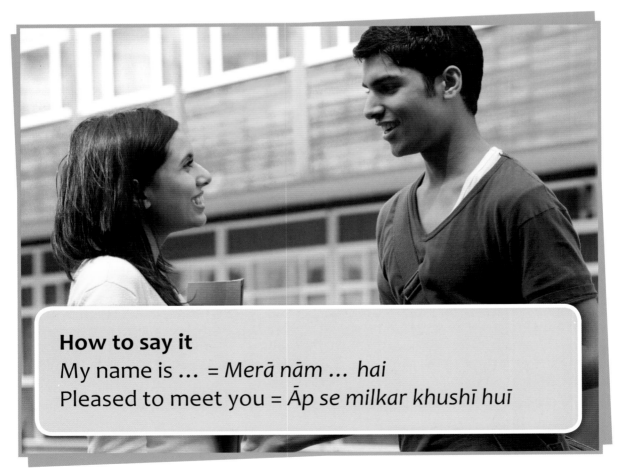

How to say it
My name is … = *Merā nām … hai*
Pleased to meet you = *Āp se milkar khushī huī*

You might also tell someone where you are from by saying "*Maĩ Pakistan se hũ*" ("I am from Pakistan"). If you make a mistake you might say "*māf karnā*" ("sorry").

Asking About Others

When greeting someone, you might say "*khush āmdīd*" ("welcome"). Then you might ask "*Āpkā nām kyā hai?*" ("What is your name?") and "*Āp kahā̃ se haĩ?*" ("Where are you from?")

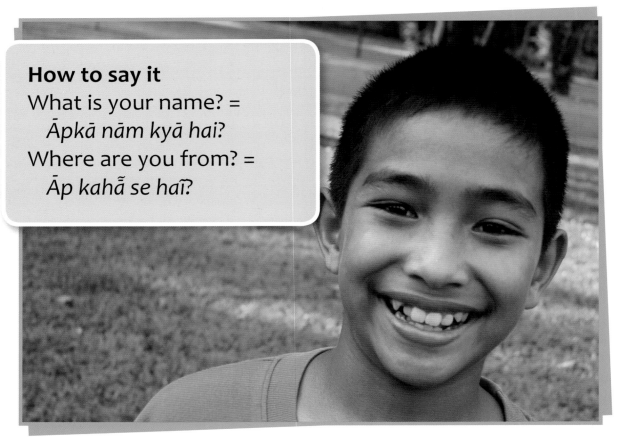

How to say it
What is your name? =
  Āpkā nām kyā hai?
Where are you from? =
  Āp kahā̃ se haĩ?

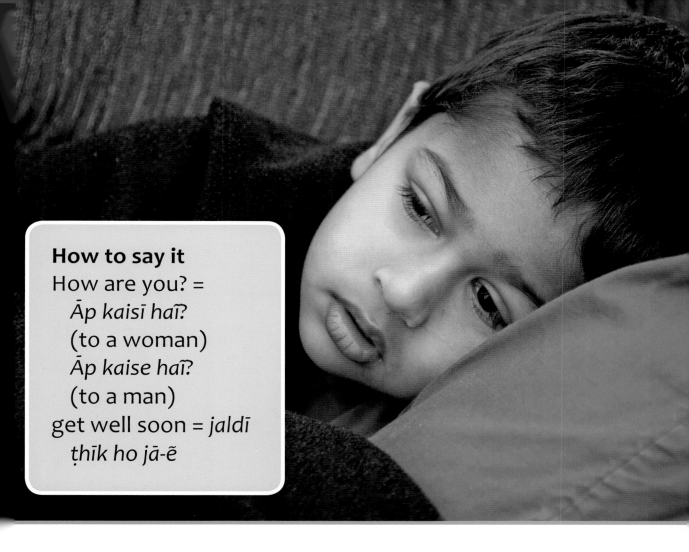

How to say it
How are you? =
  Āp kaisī haĩ?
  (to a woman)
  Āp kaise haĩ?
  (to a man)
get well soon = *jaldī
  ṭhīk ho jā-ẽ*

To say "How are you?" you would ask a woman, "*Āp kaisī haĩ?*" For a man, you would ask "*Āp kaise haĩ?*" If someone is sick, you might say "*jaldī ṭhīk ho jā-ẽ*" ("get well soon").

At Home

Some people in Pakistan live in big cities. They make their homes in apartment buildings. They have modern things like televisions and computers.

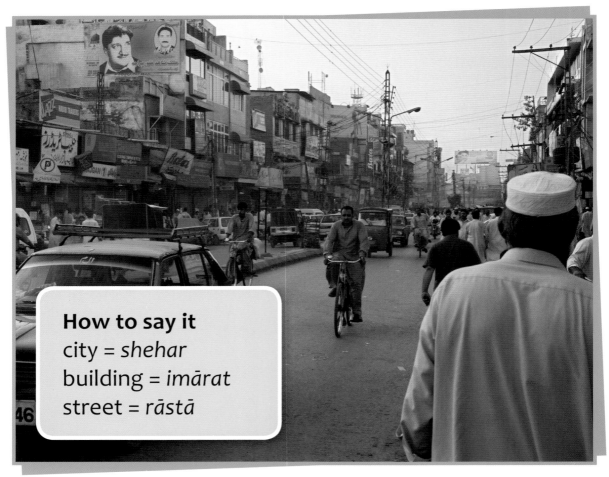

How to say it
city = *shehar*
building = *imārat*
street = *rāstā*

How to say it
home = *ghar*
door = *darwāzā*
window = *khiṛkī*

Other people in Pakistan live in villages. Some homes are made of mud or clay. They might have dirt floors. These homes might not have electricity.

Family Life

In Pakistan one house can be home to an older couple with their sons, sons' wives, unmarried daughters, and grandchildren. Most daughters live with their parents until they get married.

How to say it
father = *wālid*
mother = *wālidā*
children = *bache*

How to say it
brother = *bhāī*
sister = *behan*
fun = *mazāh*

Boys and girls play together. But when they get older, women do not usually mix with men from outside their family. Sometimes men and women sit in separate areas of restaurants.

At School

Many children in Pakistan go to school, but most pupils are boys. Throughout the country many people cannot read. The government (people who run the country) is trying to change that.

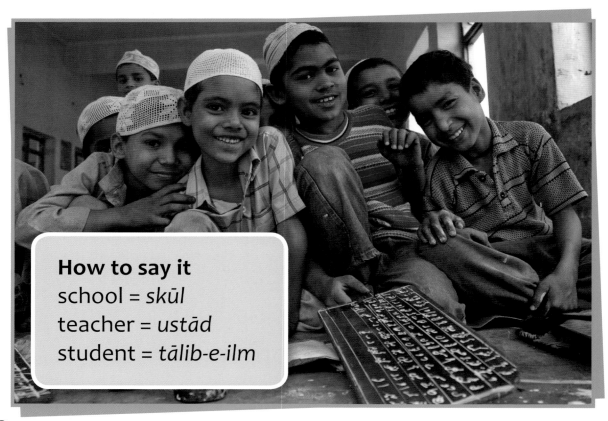

How to say it
school = *skūl*
teacher = *ustād*
student = *tālib-e-ilm*

How to say it
English = *angrezī*
history = *tārīkh*
book = *kitāb*

Pupils at schools in Pakistan study math, history, science, and English. They also learn about religion.

Sports

Cricket is the main sport of Pakistan. This game is played with bats and balls. People in Pakistan also like to play field hockey, squash, and soccer.

How to say it
ball = *gend*
run = *dauṛnā*
shoe = *jūtā*

Some people in Pakistan play polo.
There are two teams. Players ride horses
and hit a ball into the other team's goal.
A famous polo tournament is held in
Pakistan each year.

Food and Drink

Many people in Pakistan eat beef, chicken, and vegetables. *Dāl* is a popular lentil stew. Most meals also include a flat bread called *chapātī*.

How to say it
meat = *gosht*
chicken = *murghī*
lentil stew = *dāl*
flat bread = *chapātī*

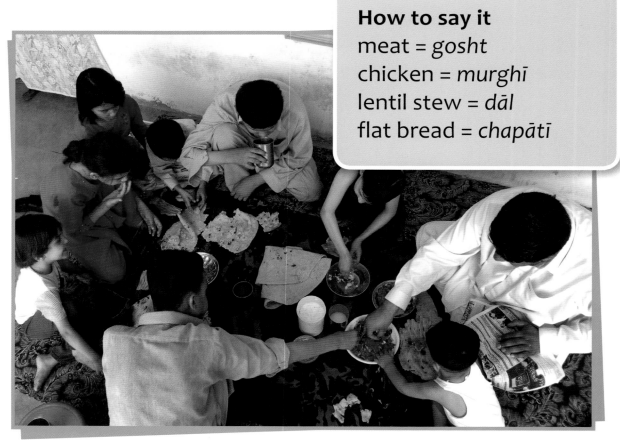

How to say it
yogurt drink = *lassī*
tea = *chāi*

Lassī is a delicious drink made from yogurt. Many people also drink *chāi*, which is a kind of tea. *Khīr* is a rice pudding made with nuts.

27

Clothes and Shopping

In Pakistan clothing is often brightly colored. Both men and women wear outfits called *salwar kamīz*. Women may also wear a scarf called a *dupatta*.

How to say it
dress = *libās*
shirt = *kamīz*
trousers = *patlūn*

How to say it
fruit = *phal*
vegetable = *sabzī*

People in Pakistan often shop in an outdoor market called a *bāzār*. They buy fresh fruit and vegetables. They may also buy rugs and blankets. Pakistan is also known for its pottery.

Pronunciation Guide

English	Urdu	Pronunciation
ball	*gend*	*gend*
book	*kitāb*	*kitaab*
brother	*bhāī*	*bhaa-ee*
building	*imārat*	*imaarat*
chicken	*murghī*	*murghee*
children	*bache*	*bachay*
city	*shehar*	*shehar*
door	*darwāzā*	*darwaazaa*
dress	*libās*	*libaas*
English	*angrezī*	*angrezee*
father	*wālid*	*waalid*
flat bread	*chapātī*	*chapaatee*
fruit	*phal*	*phal*
fun	*mazāh*	*mazaah*
game	*khel*	*khayl*
get well soon	*jaldī ṭhīk ho jā-ē*	*jaldee theek ho jaa-ay*
goodbye	*khudā hāfiz*	*khudaa haafiz*
good morning	*subha bākhair*	*subha baakhair*
goodnight	*shab bākhair*	*shab baakhair*
happiness	*khushī*	*khushee*
hat	*ṭopī*	*topee*
hello	*assalām ālekum*	*assalaam aalaykum*
history	*tārīkh*	*taareekh*
home	*ghar*	*ghar*
horse	*ghoṛā*	*ghoraa*

How are you?	Āp kaisī haĩ? (female)	Aap kaisee hai?
	Āp kaise haĩ? (male)	Aap kaisay hai?
I am from ...	Maĩ ... se hũ	Mai ... say hoo
lentil stew	dāl	daal
market	bāzār	baazaar
meat	gosht	gosht
mother	wālidā	waalidaa
My name is ...	Merā nām ... hai	Meraa naam ... hai
pajamas	pājāmā	paajaamaa
Pleased to meet you	Āp se milkar khushī huī	Aap say milkar khushee huee
rice pudding	khīr	kheer
run	dauṛnā	daurnaa
school	skūl	school
shirt	kamīz	kameez
shoe	jūtā	jootaa
sister	behan	behan
sorry	māf karnā	maaf karnaa
street	rāstā	raastaa
student	tālib-e-ilm	taalib-e-ilm
tea	chāi	chaai
teacher	ustād	ustaad
trousers	patlūn	patloon
vegetable	sabzī	sabzee
welcome	khush āmdīd	khush aamdeed
What is your name?	Āpkā nām kyā hai?	Aapkaa naam kyaa hai?
Where are you from?	Āp kahã se haĩ?	Aap kahaa say hai?
window	khiṛkī	khirkee
yogurt drink	lassī	lassee

Find Out More

Books

Roop, Peter and Connie. *A Visit to India.* Chicago: Heinemann Library, 2008.

Lynch, Emma. *We're from Pakistan.* Chicago: Heinemann, 2008.

Note to Parents and Teachers

Please use the following as a guide to pronunciation:

~ = *a nasal sound, as in the "n" in hunger*

t = *a soft "t" sound, pronounced by the tongue touching the back of the upper teeth*

ṭ = *"t" as in train*

d = *a soft "d" sound, pronounced by the tongue touching the back of the upper teeth*

r = *the Urdu "r" sound is rolled more than the English "r" sound*

ṛ = *a similar sound to "r", but the tongue flaps against the roof of the mouth. At first it can be tricky to pronounce it.*

Index